BIG NUMBERS

AND PICTURES THAT SHOW JUST HOW **BIG** THEY ARE!

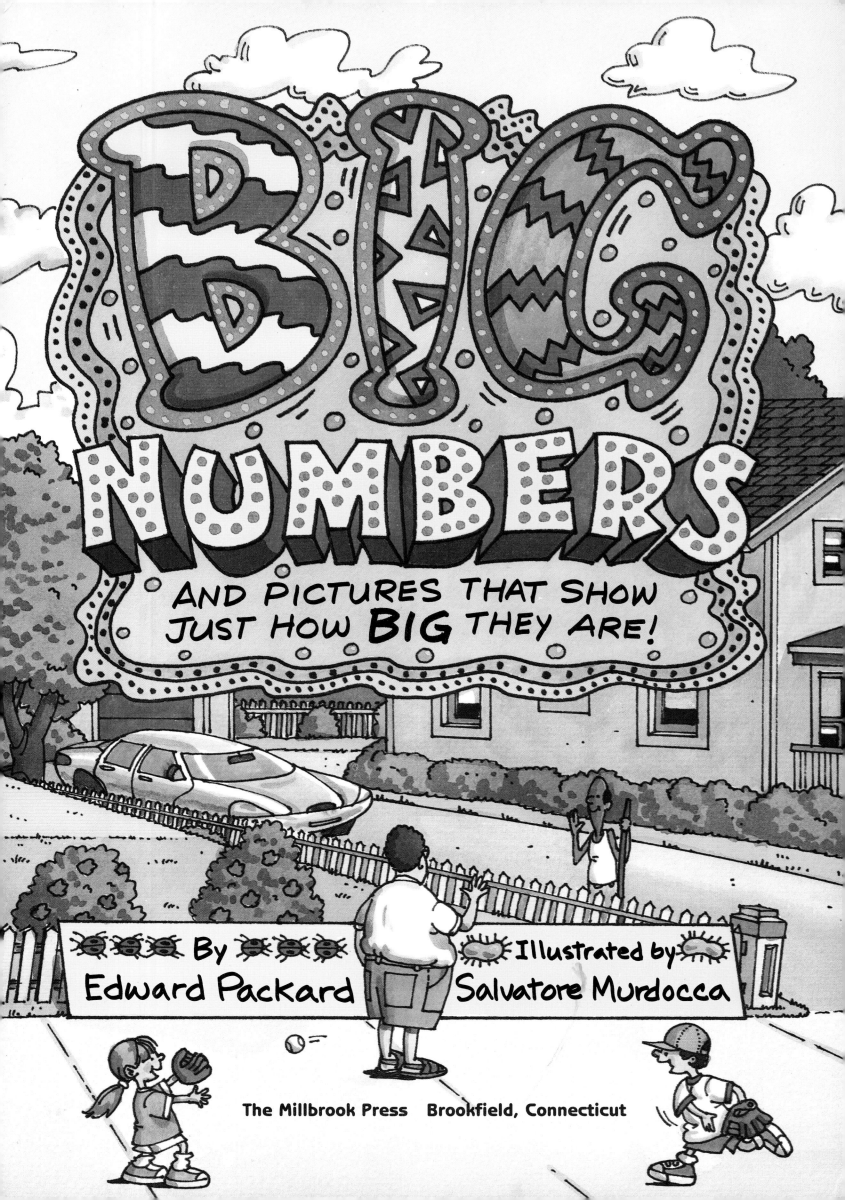

BIG

NUMBERS

AND PICTURES THAT SHOW JUST HOW **BIG** THEY ARE!

By Edward Packard

Illustrated by Salvatore Murdocca

The Millbrook Press   Brookfield, Connecticut

For
Amy,
David,
and Sam. — E.P.

To
my friend,
Victor. — S.M.

Library of Congress Cataloging-in-Publication Data

Big numbers : and pictures that show just how big they are! / by Edward Packard;
illustrated by Salvatore Murdocca.

p. cm.
Summary: Uses illustrations of exponentially increasing peas to present the concept
of numbers from one to a million, billion, trillion.
ISBN 0-7613-1570-5 (lib. bdg.)   ISBN 0-7613-1280-3 (trade) ISBN 0-7613-0938-1 (pbk.)
1. Place value (Mathematics) Juvenile literature. 2. Decimal system Juvenile literature.
[1. Decimal system. 2. Exponents (Algebra) 3. Number systems.]
I. Murdocca, Sal, ill. II. Title.
QA141.35.P33 2000
513.5'5—dc21   99-32242   CIP

Published by The Millbrook Press, Inc.
2 Old New Milford Road
Brookfield, Connecticut 06804
www.millbrookpress.com

You've seen big numbers, like

a thousand
a million
and maybe even a billion

How big are they?
How big can they get?

This book shows you.

SNIFF, SNIFF

We'll start small—with the number 1

ONE

1

One pea on a plate.

TEN

Ten is an important number because we have ten fingers and ten toes.

Ten peas on a plate.

ONE HUNDRED

Can you tell what month it will be a hundred days from now?

One hundred peas is a small helping of peas.

One hundred million peas fill up the kitchen and spill out into the dining room.

A hundred million years ago a dinosaur might have been standing in your backyard.

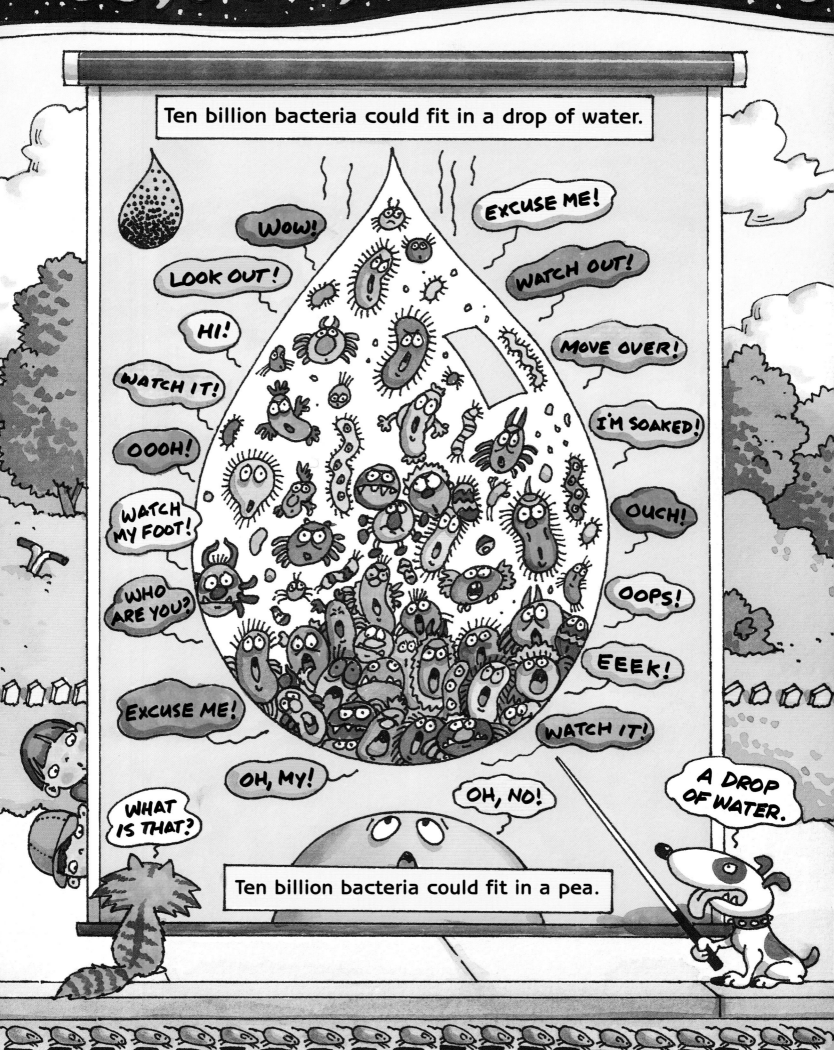

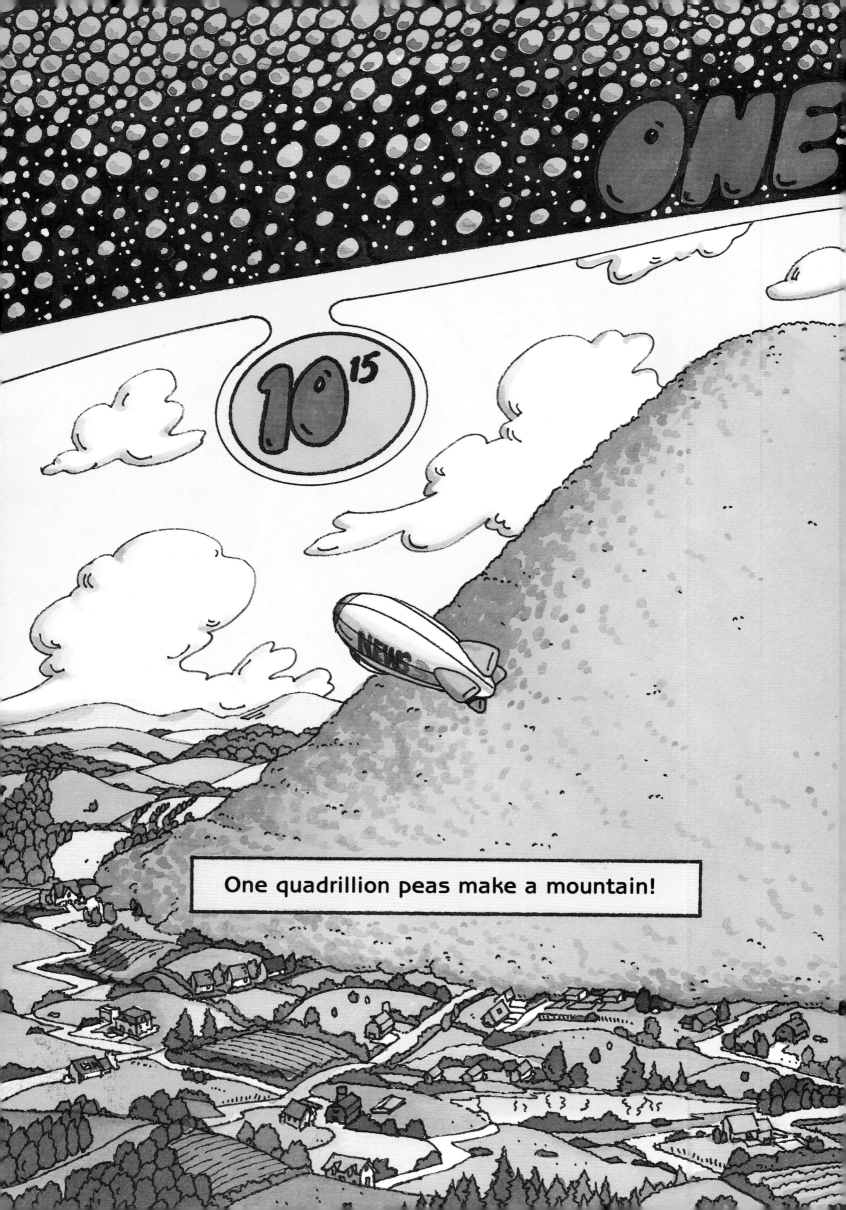

One quadrillion peas make a mountain!